A TENT, a JawBONE and a SheepskiN Rug

WRITTEN BY
Malc' Halliday

CARTOONS BY
Ian Potter

Scripture Union

© Malc' Halliday 2000
First published 2000

ISBN 1 85999 294 3

British Library Cataloguing-in-Publication Data.
A catalogue record for this book is available from the British
Library.

Printed and bound in Great Britain by Creative Print and Design
(Wales), Ebbw Vale.

WHAT'S WHERE

WHO'S WHO?

WHAT'S WHEN?

1406BC Israelites enter Canaan

1367BC Othniel

1309BC Ehud

1209BC Deborah

1162BC Gideon

1105BC Samuel born

1075BC Samson

1050BC Saul anointed king

1010BC David becomes king

WHERE'S WHERE?

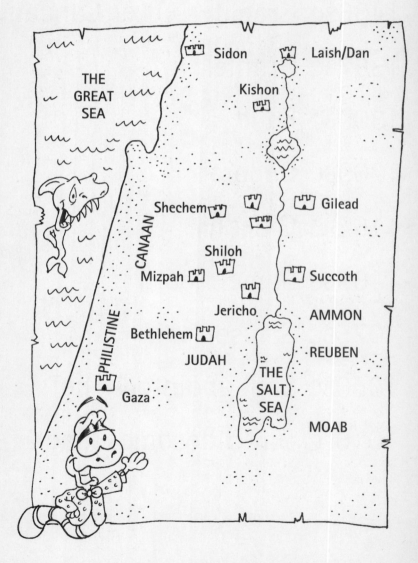

YOUR GUIDES

SHIMEI THE SMELLI

Alright! I'm Shimei. How are ya? I'd just like to say, 'Nice one for buying this book!' I'll be guiding you through the ins and outs, the ups and downs, the highs and lows, the tops and bottoms... not that there are many bottoms in here. You get the idea. Anyway, I'll be showing you around the book, and to help me with this enormous task is Benji.

BENJI THE BOOKWORM

Hi! I'm Benji – I've managed to worm my way (geddit?) into this book because Shimei is hopeless with numbers. He also smells awful, but that's another story. When you see me holding up a sign, if you like you can get your Bible out and read the 'official' version of the story.

INTRODUCTION

Hello, good evening and welcome. Nice of you to drop by. I hope you have settled yourself down comfortably and you've left all the lights on because we're about to set out on a journey that could be just a little scary (and anyway if you were sitting in the dark you wouldn't be able to read this would you?). We're going back to a time when life was rough, life was tough and, quite frankly, life was incredibly short, if you argued with the wrong people.

Many of the people in the stories which follow were in the wrong place at the right time (or should that be the other way round?). They spent a lot of time doing dastardly deeds, often beheading first and asking questions later.

WHEN YOU PUT IT LIKE THAT MAYBE YOU'RE CORRECT.

Despite this, they were good lads who loved their mothers (honestly). What's more, although they spent a lot of time fighting, they believed deep down there was more to life than how many people you killed on a Friday night. They made mistakes, they got things wrong, and at times they were downright pig-headed, but they were trying to do the things God wanted – although discovering what that was wasn't all that easy. It still isn't, come to think about it, but maybe we can pick up a hint or two along the way.

If you think you're up for it, turn the page...

JOSHUA

It had all been such a long time ago, thought Joshua as he lay on his bed, and such a lot had happened. He thought back to those early days when being Assistant Leader was challenge enough and the idea of having the top job never crossed his mind. Until...

'WHOA!'

(At this point, if this was TV, your screen would go all wavy and strange music would be heard... you can achieve the same effect by waving this book up and down, making yourself go cross-eyed and gargling the tune of any ABBA classic.)

Compared with Moses (120 years if he was a day) Joshua was just a young man and now Moses had gone. (People said he'd died but who could be sure? There was a rumour that God had taken care of the funeral arrangements, but nobody knew for certain.) He had been told it was his job to get the people into the Promised Land. God had said, 'It will be yours,' and even after forty years wandering about, there were those who said, 'We'll get there in the end.' Of course they'd had their chance once before. Moses had sent his spies mincing into Canaan (they were mince-spies! Hahaha!) and when they came back what stories they had to tell!

Giant fruit, abundant food, ideal 'family of God' location and, oh yes, quite a lot of nasty unpleasant-looking people who gave the impression they would spear, disembowel and generally mutilate first, and not even bother to ask questions later. The verdict was simple: let's leave them to it. And they did and carried on wandering around for forty years. But then Joshua sent his boys in to have a scout round (they were boy scouts!) and they came back with tales of wonder and opulence and generally good things, but also with the news 'The Lord has given you the whole country'. Joshua took heart – yes the opposition were ugly, they were fierce, they made Arnold Schwarzenegger look like Mr Bean, but Joshua had a secret weapon – he knew that God was on their side, so this time they were going for it. The people surrounded Jericho and waited for the battle plan, the giving out of weapons, and the

secret
strategies. Imagine
their surprise when
Josh told them God's
instructions. 'Walk
round the city.' Thinking
it was a limbering-up exercise, off they went without a murmur.
It wasn't just soldiers, either. Hidden away within their ranks was
a little group of priests who had formed their own brass band
(called the Desert Welly Foot Stompers, or something) who, while
everyone marched, were playing away fit to burst. All those
favourite tunes from long ago, 'Sphinx shoe shuffle', 'I've got the
"Pharoah's being really mean to us and I can't make any more
bricks" blues', 'Red Sea Rag' – that kind of thing.

Then Joshua told them to do the same the next day, and the day after that and... well, you get the idea. They did it for six whole days. When they woke on the seventh day they expected more of the same, but Joshua knew that seven days of silent marching can make one weak (one week... geddit?) so he went for Phase Two.

14

This time they were allowed to march *and* shout *and* blow their own trumpets – what a leader: such vision, such strategy, such barmy ideas. Except this barmy idea paid off – the shout went up and the walls came down. In later centuries, opera singers managed

to do a similar trick with a single note and a wine glass, but nobody has ever quite matched the achievements of *Joshua and his Howling Hebrews*.

Now the land was theirs and people wanted their share of the property. Moses had begun sharing it all out, but there were still a few bits unclaimed and Joshua was the one to sort it out. To get it right really needed the wisdom of Solomon, but he hadn't been born yet so Josh just had to rely on God.[1] Things seemed to go well but now Joshua wasn't quite as active as he had been, he couldn't run for buses any more and his doctor had

---

[1] Handy-Hint Corner no 427: always a good idea to rely on God, whatever the situation.

begun to say it was a set of wooden dentures like his Gran's or jelly and Lucozade for the rest of his natural. He was only 110 but he knew his number was up. But there was one thing he wanted to say before he took a final ride on the ferris wheel of life (Alton Towers, I mean). He gathered the leaders around him and reminded them that everything they had, everything they enjoyed was all down to God so they weren't to forget him. 'The Lord your God has been fighting for you,' he said. There were murmurs and grunts and cries of 'Hear, hear'. 'Choose God,' said Joshua. 'Whatever you do, whatever decisions there are to make, whatever situations you face, choose God!' 'We will, we will,' said the crowd, hoping this was the right answer and shutting up a troublemaker at the back who kept asking, 'Has he left a will? Who did he leave his money to?' Joshua wasn't sure they had understood, so his last words were to urge them to 'Really choose

We really, really choose God
We rearly, really choose God
We rearly, rearly choose God
We rarely, rearly choose God
We rarely, rarely choose God

God.' 'We really, really choose God,' was the chorus echoing in his ears as he slipped away, and I expect some of them really, really meant it. And so for a while the motto of God's people was 'WE REALLY, REALLY CHOOSE GOD'. But you know how it is: years go by, things get copied out badly, somebody mishears what somebody else says and soon the motto sewn neatly into every Israelite schoolboy's blazer was:

'WE RARELY RARELY CHOOSE GOD'.

Who would have thought changing a couple of letters would have made all that much difference? But, as we will see, things were taking place in the nation that if Joshua had still been alive for, he'd have been turning in his grave.

18

OTHNIEL

JUDGES 3:7-11

The Israelites suffered from short-term memory loss. Not something that afflicts many of us. If bad things happen, we remember them and don't go round repeating our mistakes. The Israelites weren't like that. They suffered from short-term memory loss and were always making the same mistakes over and over again. They suffered from short-term memory loss and were always making the same mistakes over and over again. If they did something wrong then instead of learning the lesson, they just did it all over again. This was because the Israelites suffered from short-term memory loss.

SHORT-TERM MEMORY LOSS! WHAT'S THAT?

CAN'T REMEMBER!

CAN'T REMEMBER WHAT?

ERM...?

WHAT A GREAT NEW LAND!

ISN'T GOD GREAT!

HEY! LOOK AT THESE GUYS!

HI! WHAT'S GOING ON?

WE'RE WORSHIPPING THESE STONES! DO JOIN US!

THIS IS BRILL, BUT WHAT ABOUT GOD?

WHO?

By about 1200 BC. the people of Israel were mixing with the Canaanites, the Hittites, the Amorites and the Perizzites: in fact they hung out with just about any rock band that happened to be passing through (except Metallica). The problem was they didn't just get to know these people but started to be like them: eat their food, marry their women, worship their gods and wear ripped jeans. God wasn't at all pleased about this. After all, if you were Creator of heaven and earth, Supreme Ruler of the Universe and the One True God and people decided they preferred worshipping a pile of rocks and a bit of a tree trunk, wouldn't you be a bit miffed?

So God allowed the Israelites to be conquered by the King of Mesopotamia. His name was Cushan Rishathaim of Aran Naharaim. This name had the advantage of allowing you into the palace and overthrowing the king and soldiers while the butler was still announcing you.

'NOT QUITE THE KIND OF CONQUERING WE HAD IN MIND.'

For eight years CR (as he was known to his friends) ruled the people of Israel. By which time the Israelites remembered it didn't have to be this way: so they asked God to help. Now God didn't suffer from short-term memory loss: he knew what the Israelites were like, he knew they would probably forget him again, but he also knew he loved them and wanted things to go well for them.

God looked around for someone to help. It had to be someone who could handle big names, someone who wouldn't be fazed by a king whose name looked like an explosion on a Scrabble board. There was such a man among the people of Judah. His uncle was Caleb Ben Jephunneh and in his younger days he had captured Kiriath-Sepher (which was also called

'Debir' – if you try saying its original name you'll understand why). Here was a man who could leap the alphabetical mine fields of long names with a single bound. His name was OTHNIEL. I know it's not a very long name but try saying it slowly. However, it *is* an anagram of THE LION which can't be bad!

He came, he saw, he conquered, a long time before Julius Caesar had the same idea! Of course he had God to help him, so giving Othniel all the credit would be a bit like you being given a bravery award because you happened to be there when the local police captured a notorious criminal. Nevertheless, Othniel was the hero of the day and forty years of peace followed.

21

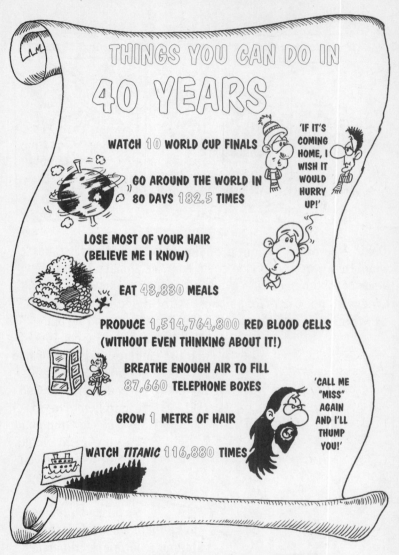

THINGS YOU CAN DO IN
40 YEARS

WATCH 10 WORLD CUP FINALS

'IF IT'S COMING HOME, I WISH IT WOULD HURRY UP!'

GO AROUND THE WORLD IN 80 DAYS 182.5 TIMES

LOSE MOST OF YOUR HAIR (BELIEVE ME I KNOW)

EAT 43,830 MEALS

PRODUCE 1,514,764,800 RED BLOOD CELLS (WITHOUT EVEN THINKING ABOUT IT!)

BREATHE ENOUGH AIR TO FILL 87,660 TELEPHONE BOXES

'CALL ME "MISS" AGAIN AND I'LL THUMP YOU!'

GROW 1 METRE OF HAIR

WATCH *TITANIC* 116,880 TIMES

It was also enough time to forget what God had done for you. And with a regularity that borders on the monotonous, Year 40 was followed by year 41 'dun dun daaaaaaah!'

WHAT WAS THAT?

There's an important thing to remember here, and if you give me a moment I'll try and remember it. The people had made a bad beginning in Canaan. It wasn't simply that they worshipped all these bits of metal and wood and ignored God (although that was pretty serious). It was even more basic than that. You see the false gods shouldn't have been around to worship. God had told the people that the first thing they had to do was get rid of them – but they didn't. Centuries later, Jesus said something to his followers about getting rid of the things that cause us to sin. If only the Israelites had got it right to start with, maybe there wouldn't be this endless pile of failure, evil and disobedience going round and round – like your dirty socks in the washing machine.

Round and round – that's it! That's what you have to remember: the Spin Cycle – that's what the Israelites were locked into.

EHUD
YEAR 41

The short-term memory loss principle came into operation again in year 41. (If you can't remember what that is, look back at the story of Robbie Williams, no that's not it, uuhm, Othniel. Err – if you can't remember where that is, are you sure you're not an Israelite?) This time the people were

JUDGES 3:12-30

overthrown by a king named Eglon. This is an anagram of 'no leg' and would have been quite funny had he, indeed, been Long John Silver. However, not only was he up to quota in the leg department, he had an abundance of leg. He had an abundance of everything. Eglon was bonny, big-boned, a little on the plump side, large for his age, a growing lad, calorifically challenged – oh to heck with it... Eglon was FAT (very fat – huge, enormous). He came and set up base in Palm City. It used to be known as Jericho, but since Joshua and his gang had passed through some years ago, the palms were just about the only things left standing. However, in choosing this as his centre of operations, Eglon may well have made his first big mistake (aside from refusing to stop at fourteen helpings during mealtimes). Joshua had said that if anybody rebuilt Jericho he would be cursed – and he had been right about the walls falling down.

It took longer for the Israelites to realise that God might want things to be a bit different – eighteen years this time – but at last they shouted out for help. They didn't need to shout, of course. God was closer than they knew and, once again, he wanted to help.

If Othniel was more of your 'straight in, kill, clear up' sort of guy, the man God chose for the job this time was more of a '007, licensed to kill and do it all in secret' chap. He wasn't perhaps an obvious choice. For a start he was left-handed – not necessarily good news. Throughout history left-handed people have had it tough and Israel 1160 BC was no exception. Take a look at these charts:

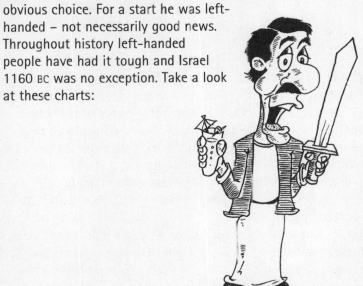

THE GOOD NEWS FOR RIGHT-HANDED PEOPLE
Right means correct, proper
Sensible people are in their 'right mind'
People are blessed by God's right hand (Isaiah 62:8,9)
Enemies are destroyed by God's right hand (Exodus 15:6)
At God's right hand are pleasures for ever more (Psalm 16:11)

THE BAD NEWS FOR LEFT-HANDED PEOPLE
The Latin for left hand is SINISTER
On average left-handed people die younger
Michelangelo and Charlie Chaplin were left-handed (but so was Jack the Ripper)
A 'left-handed compliment' means an insult
The people of Israel referred to left-handed people as 'deformed in the right hand'
In library books left-handed people are classified under 'special needs'

Not really good news, is it? But in fact, in good espionage style, being left-handed was the best secret weapon Ehud had.

He disguised himself as a messenger with his sword hidden along his right leg. Of course any self-respecting paranoid king would be looking for a weapon on the left side (right-handers wore their swords there so as to grab them easily) and would not have noticed Ehud's little secret – unless walking along with eighteen inches of iron strapped to his leg made him walk with a pronounced limp.

Ehud came with a present for the king. We don't know what the present was but – and I'm just guessing here – it could well have been something edible. *Anything* edible would have made Eglon happy! Having delivered the gift, Ehud went on his way but this was all part of the plan for this Hebrew master spy. After a while he came back and told the king, 'I've a secret message for you.' Of course Eglon wanted to know what the message was, but

Ehud said, 'I can't tell you with everyone around, it's a secret,' and gave Eglon a knowing look. Eglon sent all his servants away by shouting 'Quiet!' (Very strange these tyrant-kings. Presumably if he had wanted them to stop talking he would have shouted 'Get out!') Ehud came nearer the king, all alone now. 'I've a message from God,' he said, which wasn't really a lie (after all isn't God's Word like a two-edged sword?). Eglon soon discovered that it was, as Ehud thrust his sword in

I HAVE A MESSAGE FROM GOD.

through the flesh, through the subcutaneous fat, through the sub-subcutaneous fat, through the sub- sub- sub-... (This was one very fat king.) The sword went on and on until it disappeared altogether. Ehud thought of reaching in after it, but changed his mind when he saw the gore, putrid body tissue, wobbly bits, blood and undigested portions of yesterday's dinner that were pouring out of the wound. Then, like any good spy, he made his escape, locking the doors behind him and not even leaving a farewell note.

Eglon's guards came back thinking Ehud had had time to deliver the message. They waited outside the doors deciding the king was probably using the facilities, and of the things the guards didn't want to lay eyes on, the king on the toilet was top of the list. They waited and they waited and they waited until

they couldn't wait any longer (in every sense). They debated among themselves what they should do. Should someone climb the outside walls and get in through the window? Could they get a battering ram and smash the doors down? Then one of the guards (clearly officer material) had a bright idea. 'Why don't we just get the key and open the door?' he said. So that's what they did and found the king had expired, drawn his final breath, ceased to be, snuffed it, fallen off his twig, shuffled off this mortal coil. Oh, okay, he was dead. And fat. In fact he was dead and dead fat.

Meanwhile, Ehud was blowing his own trumpet. Well, you'd have been proud if you'd managed such a neat trick. He could imagine the headlines in the Israeli Daily Star:

ISRAELI DAILY STAR

EXCLUSIVE

FAT CAT GOES SPLAT

– AND THAT'S THAT

BUILDERS DEMOLISH WALLS TO REMOVE BODY

PALACE CHEFS CELEBRATE

CIRCUS FINDS NEW HOME IN EGLON'S GIANT VEST

CAKE COMPANY FACES STOCK MARKET CRASH

The Israelites heard the trumpet and came running. With the news that Eglon was gone, they rallied around Ehud and went after the Moabites, killing ten thousand of them before the rest took the hint and turned tail and ran.

Things could have looked tricky for Ehud at his next kit inspection, trying to explain where his sword had got to. But since he was now the national hero and leader of his people nobody dared make an issue of it.

So it was that peace came to the land, and this time there wasn't a hint of trouble for eighty years. But you know what's coming next don't you? After year 80 there was year 81.

SHAMGAR

'NOW KEEP THIS TO YOURSELF...'

Now keep this to yourselves, but our next contender for Israel's latest Super-Hero and National Deliverer wasn't even a Hebrew. We can tell this from his name: Shamgar – you won't find that in the Israelite book of baby names. However, if you suspect that his mum and dad had picked a foreign name just to be different you should also know that he was called 'son of Amath'. Amath wasn't his dad but a pagan goddess. Believe me, this man had come over from the opposition. Still, when you need rescuing, 'any port in a storm' as my old granny used to say (mind you she was bonkers). And for those who suspected he might simply be a spy waiting to double-cross the Israelites, he went out and killed six hundred of his former countrymen with a pointed stick. So just remember next time someone tells you it's rude to point, it can be downright dangerous too.

JUDGES 3:31

Shamgar, like all the other judges, died but he achieved immortality by appearing in a song some years later. A song we still have in our Bibles to this day, although you won't find it in your hymn books.

DEBORAH and BARAK

Well, once again, God's people forgot about him and once again they did their own thing and, surprise surprise, once again they woke up one morning and found they had been conquered by a foreign king (the more astute may notice a bit of a pattern emerging here).

'WAKE UP, DARLING, WE'RE BEING INVADED AGAIN.'

King Jabin of Canaan was rough, he was tough, he had 900 chariots (and he knew how to use them) and what's more he didn't like the Israelites very much. In fact, he had a bit of a grudge against them, as one of his ancestors had been given a kick up the ego some years before by Joshua (quite painful!). So it was that for twenty years, with the help of his trusty side-kick Sisera, he was cruel, violent and didn't care a bit.

Meanwhile, far away under a distant palm tree, sat a judge. Now so far you may have noticed that the judges have been more your 'let's go to war and do dastardly deeds' type than your 'it's the view of this court that you should be jolly sorry for what you've done' type. Well this judge was the business:

dispensing advice and wisdom, settling arguments and dissecting the finer points of Israelite law. This judge was a leader like judges before and to cap it all was a prophet into the bargain. Judge, leader and prophet: three of Israel's top jobs and one person doing them all... amazing. The toppest job of all was, of course, priest. And however wonderful this person was, they were never going to reach those dizzy heights because they weren't allowed to. And why weren't they allowed to? (Wait for it... this one's a real shocker.) The judge was a WOMAN.

'I KNOW IT MIGHT SEEM SHOCKING AND SEXIST AND ALL THAT KIND OF THING BUT THINGS WERE DIFFERENT IN THOSE DAYS.'

Yes, that's right, God surprised everyone again by going for the unlikely candidate. Judge Deborah was the one to sort out Jabin and his chariots. She sent for a man named Barak (pronounced 'Barak') to tell him that God had a cunning plan: Barak was to take 10,000 of his mates and set off to Kishon to deal with Sisera once and for all. Now Barak was not the bravest man in the world (even with 10,000 soldiers behind him), so he told Deborah he'd only go if she went with him. It might just have been a complicated way of asking her for a date, but since he was already married it's more likely he was thinking 'If I'm going to risk my life the least she can do is come with me'. With a sigh, Deborah got up from under the palm tree and went off with Barak, muttering something about how he'd had the chance to be the hero of this story and blown it.

Barak went up into the mountains and Sisera took his men (and his chariots) down into the river valley. It was summer and the river had dried up, so

the ground was just right for racing chariots along and mowing down bolshy Israelites.

However, things didn't quite work out the way Sisera had expected. By the end of the day the Canaanite soldiers were all dead, and Sisera was running for his life.

How had it all happened? Deborah, thinking about things the next day, wrote a little song to mark the occasion, which went something like this:[1]

God's people decided to fight
To put the Canaanite army to flight
Deb'rah said, 'Barak go get 'em
Escape don't you let 'em'
Barak thought, 'Hang on now that can't be right.'

Barak said, 'If what you say's true
I know what a bloke's gotta do
But Deborah,' he said,
'If I won't end up dead
You won't mind coming along too.'

Deborah got up with no warning
And said, as Barak started yawning,
'OK, I'll come along
But as you'll find from this song
You'll be sorry for this in the morning.'

The Canaanite army was vast
The chariots couldn't 'alf go fast
The enemy crowds
Saw gathering clouds
And thought that the shower would soon pass.

The rain just kept dropping and dropping
Which caught all the Canaanites hopping
Driving was no good

---

[1]The translation is a loose rendition of the original – one of the oldest bits of the Bible.

They just slid in the mud
And suddenly found themselves stopping.

Barak's men were on them like a flash
The enemy had made quite a hash

They were dead, every man
So Sisera ran
Saying, ' 'Scuse me, no time, got to dash.'

The song goes on like this for some time because, for the Israelites, this victory at Kishon was not the end of the story, as we shall see.

Sisera ran off looking for someone to hide him, someone who was a friend, someone who could be trusted: he chose Jael's tent. How wrong could you be? Jael's husband was friends with Sisera's boss (remember him – King Jabin??), so Sisera thought he had found the perfect hiding place. Certainly Jael welcomed him and offered him hospitality, which in those days meant you promised to look after your visitor while they were with you. Unfortunately Jael had missed a couple of sessions at her etiquette evening school classes

and so didn't seem to grasp fully what her duties were, beyond offering the first drink and a plate of nibbles. She was also a little hard of hearing it seems, so that when Sisera said, 'Keep an eye out,' she *thought* he said, 'Poke my eye out'. And so, while he was asleep, that's what she set out to do, armed only with a heavy hammer and a tent peg. Mind you she made a right mess of that... missed the eye completely and the tent peg went right through Sisera's head, pinning him to the ground. Not that it mattered very much because he wasn't going anywhere – ever again. However, this did lead to some problems as the following conversation shows (it's not very polite but believe me you can learn a lot ear-wigging at tent flaps).

OH RACHEL, WILL YOU
LOOK AT THE STAIN ON THIS! I'VE
TRIED EVERYTHING BUT NOTHING SHIFTS
BLOOD. MIND YOU, NOTHING SHIFTED HIM TILL
I TOOK THE PEG OUT...HMMMM? OH, HE'S OUT
THE BACK. I HAVEN'T WORKED OUT WHAT TO DO
WITH HIM YET. I CAN HARDLY SEND HIM HOME, CAN I,
WITH A LITTLE LABEL ROUND HIS NECK 'SORRY FOR THE
INCONVENIENCE'?... WELL, I HAD TO HIDE HIM. I'VE HAD
HIS MUM ROUND HERE THREE TIMES. SHE'S HAD HIS TEA
ON A LOW LIGHT SINCE A WEEK LAST THURSDAY AND
CAN'T THINK WHERE HE'S GOT TO. I'M THINKING OF
WEAVING A RUG TO COVER THE WORST BITS. DO YOU
WANT SOME MORE GOAT'S MILK? TRY A BISCUIT.
YES, I MADE THEM MYSELF... AND YES, I WASHED
MY HANDS FIRST... HONESTLY SOME PEOPLE,
ONE LITTLE SLIP OF THE HAMMER AND
NOBODY TRUSTS YOU...

Despite these little domestic problems, it was a good result for Israel: two women became national heroes, Barak did a good job (although he got none of the credit) and forty years of peace followed. But as surely as night follows day, spring follows winter and one bus follows on right behind another, so forty years were followed by year ٤٢.

GIDEON

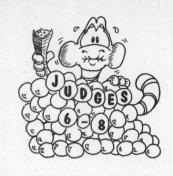

It was quiet in the winepress.
Cramped but quiet. Cramped but
quiet and, more importantly, safe.

When Gideon started work on his dad's farm, he
looked forward to working in the open air, enjoying
the great outdoors, communing with nature
(whatever that means). He did not expect
to find himself squashed into a winepress
threshing wheat. However, since the
Midianites had invaded, open-air
farming had become something of a
short-lived novelty. If it was an animal,
the Midianites would have it; if it was
growing they'd destroy it. In fact
most of the members of the Ophrah
Young Farmers' Club had hung up

TRUST IN GOD

their wellies and taken to the hills to hide in the caves.

QUIT YELLING AND GET IN HERE FOR YER DINNER.

There would be the occasional lone voice trying to remind the people why it had all come to this – why the land of plenty had become the land of tyranny – a prophet shouting out that the people had turned their backs on God so what did they expect. But nobody paid much attention. Mainly because they were either hiding in caves or winepresses.

Suddenly the lid of the winepress flew open and a cheery angelic voice shouted out, 'Oi Braveheart, the Lord is with you!'[1]

Gideon resisted the temptation to say, 'Well, no wonder it's so crowded in here,' and simply responded with the line, intended to be devastatingly withering, 'Oh yeah?' But his cheery visitor was not to be daunted for a moment. He had come to give Gideon a job and it had nothing to do with wheat, winepresses or anything else beginning with a 'w'. It was to do with warfare. God wanted

---

[1] Or something like that – I'm afraid that although I swim like a fish, I speak Hebrew like one too.

Gideon to get rid of the Midianites. This did not make Gideon dance with excitement. For a star,t there was no room in the winepress and, secondly, he was the weediest member of a weedy tribe so the whole thing weally wouldn't wash.[3] But God was not going to be thwarted. As far as he was concerned the answer was simple. He was going to help Gideon, so where was the problem?

Gideon wanted proof. He'd be in a fine mess if he listened to every passing stranger who said he'd come with a message from God. So he went off to make supper while the angel thought about it. Bread and goat was on the menu. It wasn't much, but given the frequency of the Midianite raids they were lucky to still have the goat (and the bread). Gideon prepared it beautifully and laid it out on a

---

[3] That's enough w's – Ed.

rock in front of the angel who simply said, 'So you want proof, eh?' At that, the rock burst into flames, and so did the food

which then disappeared (just like the angel). Suddenly Gideon was convinced, and in an attempt to make up for all the years spent ignoring God, he built him an altar. Mind you, he had nothing to sacrifice on it 'cos the angel had just made his last goat vanish.

His dad, Joash, however, still had a couple of bulls and God had plans for them. He wanted Gideon to sacrifice them, not on his little altar (lovely though it was), but to build another altar in the middle of town, where the altars to the Midianite gods like Baal stood, and sacrifice the bulls. Of course, as God pointed out, he'd have to destroy the pagan altars first. 'Too right,' thought Gideon, 'and there's something else I'll have to do. Wait until it's dark, and with any luck, no one will know it was me.'

Gideon wasn't the best person for the role of Urban Guerrilla[4] but trying to keep it all a secret didn't matter much anyway. The people soon found out who it was and came to get him. But his dad came to the rescue, telling the crowds to let Baal sort his son out if he was so wonderful. Mind you, this was probably before he knew his son had liberated his bulls. It might be a different story when he found out.

When the crowd had calmed down, they were quite impressed with this little chap who had taken on the might of the Midianites. They decided to give him a big name. However, since those few who could actually spell the name couldn't say it, very few people ever called him

THAT GIDEON, SUCH A MODEST CHAP.

NEVER ONE TO BLOW HIS OWN TRUMPET.

---

[4] Guerrilla (bang, bang) not Gorilla (oooh, oooh, oooh).

Jerubbaal (pronounced 'Gideon').

Meanwhile, the word had got out that there was a potential rebellion brewing and the Midianites weren't having any of it – if there was going to be an uprising, they were going to sit on it sharpish like and so they gathered in Jezreel. Imagine Gideon's surprise when, in response to this, he found himself standing up and blowing a trumpet to gather his friends to fight. He couldn't quite believe he had done it, but it was too late because the troops started arriving.

There was quite a crowd but, on the basis that no general ever suffered by recruiting too many troops, he sent out word to the tribes around and more and more came to join in the fight. This should have been enough to give Gideon confidence, but at the back of his mind was the niggling thought that if it all went wrong it wouldn't be God that these tribes would blame. So he thought he'd better let God show him again that he really was the brains behind this plan. He searched around for something really impossible that only God would be able to do: unscrambling eggs, opening a tin of beans with a banana, explaining the rules of cricket. All these were rejected in favour

of Gideon's final plan which involved putting wool out on the floor overnight and having dew fall only on the wool. Well, this was easy-peasy stuff to God, but still Gideon was looking for a loophole so he asked God to do the same trick the other way round. This was not a problem – in fact the only problem was Gideon's: was he going to trust God or not? Well, Gideon decided to take the risk. A decision helped by the fact that he now had 32,000 soldiers waiting to join him on his crusade. However,

'GO!'

God wanted to make sure that the people knew he was the one who was going to sort things out and, just in case an army of 32,000 seemed a bit much, he told Gideon he could send all the scared ones home

IS IT SAFE TO GO, MR GIDEON SIR?

(Gideon was not allowed to join them!). Twenty-two thousand
didn't need asking twice (and the other ten thousand were
probably too scared to admit they were scared). But still God
thought this was a bit much, so he told Gideon to send the
remaining soldiers down to the river to drink. Nine thousand
seven hundred bent straight down and slurped the water (their

mothers must have dragged them up). On the basis that this was
asking for someone to creep up behind you and push you in, they
were sent home too. There were only three hundred, left so
Gideon knew now that he had to trust God (but it wasn't easy).

Night fell (crash, bang, wallop) and Gideon got the green
light to fight and a bit of a nudge from one of his assistants,
Purah, who had spent a fun-packed evening skulking round the
enemy camp, listening to other people's conversations. (Just
exactly how many things do people in the Bible do that well-
brought up people aren't supposed to do?... Make a list!) In the
main, the Midianites were not saying 'Girlie Gideon and his three
hundred toy soldiers... kid's play!' No, they were worried. One of
the guards had had a dream. While asleep, he had seen a loaf
bouncing down into the camp, scattering the people and tents as
it went. 'Crumbs!' said the other guards who heard the story.
They didn't know what it meant but something told told them it
wasn't that Gideon would be inviting them all round for a picnic

when the battle was over. Something was going on and they suspected the day was not going to end with a victory parade, and them being hailed as heroes.

Gideon got his men and armed them with – guess what? From this list what would you give to people about to go into battle:

a) Bows and arrows

b) Sticks and stones (to break their bones)

c) Swords and other nasty pointed things

d) A trumpet and a jar with a torch inside

e) An AK47 semi-automatic machine gun?

If you answered d) then you are clearly getting the hang of the history of this peculiar people (and I mean peculiar). If you answered a) to c) or e)... well, good try, but you don't win a coconut.

Just before midnight, the three groups of one hundred men each blew their trumpets and smashed their jars to let the torches burn bright. That was enough for the Midianites, and they panicked, attacking anybody and everybody. Since Gideon's gang was still outside the camp, this meant they fought one another and they ran and ran and ran.

'KEEP YOUR HEAD ON! I JUST WANT TO... ERM CHAT!'

Gideon set off in pursuit, calling for reinforcements from the other Israelite tribes as he went. Everybody wanted to be in on the action, including the people of Ephraim, but somehow they didn't get asked. We don't know why: somehow Gideon just missed them off the guest list. However, they joined in anyway, chopping off a few heads here and there, including a couple of Midianite chieftains – so all in all not a bad day's work. Not everybody was helpful. The leaders of Succoth wouldn't give succour, so when Gideon had beaten the Midianites, he came back and beat them too (with thorns and briars – ouch!). The last of the Midianite leaders, Zebah and Zalumna, made the mistake of saying to Gideon: 'Come and have a go if you think you're hard enough!' Unfortunately, the sarcasm was wasted on Gideon, who went and did just that. At the end of the day Gideon was a hero and the people wanted him to be king of Israel, but Gideon knew better – God was to be their king and no one else – so he refused.

However, he was still a bit dim in some ways. Instead of being made king, he let the people give him all the jewellery they had captured from the Midianites (nose studs, eyebrow rings etc), which he turned into an idol. Perhaps it was a joke, perhaps it was the only thing he knew how to make, whatever, it didn't help the people get the message that there was only one God to be worshipped and trusted. Although there was peace in Israel

'OH! WHAT A NICE IDOL!'

for a long time, there was trouble brewing. Gideon didn't help by cheating on his wife. Result: a son named Abimelech – remember that name. In any language, it's pronounced T–R–O–U–B–L–E.

JOTHAM AND ABIMELECH

Gideon had showed what was possible
if people trusted God. Now, by this
stage you will have got used to the
way the Israelites ignore every good
example they have ever seen and do
their own thing, whenever and
however they can. However, in the
next stage of our trip through the
murkier corners of
the Old Testament, it
was not in Israel
that the trouble
started. Oh no. The
Israelites were just
getting on with their
lives, but down in
Shechem something nasty was stirring.

Shechem was not really part of Israel, but it had always been
a friendly neighbour. Now all that was about to change and the
'something nasty' who was about to make the change was called
Abimelech (pronounced 'Power-crazed mad fool'). Gideon was his
dad but, (as we have already mentioned) unlike his other
brothers, his mum had not been Gideon's wife.
When the land was divided Abimelech had ended
up with the scraggly bits. Maybe he felt shunned,
left out in the cold, unloved
by the rest of his family.
Whatever the matter was,
he set about making up for
things in a BIG way. He
didn't just want to be the

JUDGES
9:1-57

SHECHEM

judge in some far-flung corner of the kingdom. He wanted the top job. He wanted to be king.

Now when it comes to getting on in life, a boy's best friend is his mum and, sure enough, Abimelech's mum went round Shechem persuading people that having one ruler would be much better, and she happened to know just the chap (guess who?). Persuaded by this and, no doubt, thinking that if there was going to be a king it was better to be in his good books, the men of Shechem had a whip-round so that Abimelech could hire a bunch of assassins to get rid of the seventy sons of Gideon (he'd been busy). They took the money and did the job. However, they did allow one son, Jotham, to escape. Whether or not Abimelech got a refund because of this slip up we will never know. Suffice to say that Jotham was free, and was not going to keep quiet about what was going on. So it was that during Abimelech's coronation party, he popped up shouting, 'I want to tell you a story,' and this is the story he told.

The people started to wonder what the story meant. Slowly, a whisper went round the gathered crowds. 'He's talking about us! He's saying it's a mistake to make Abimelech king and we'll be in big trouble... How dare he? Let's get the little...' But by this time Jotham had done a runner – and who can blame him?

'Ha-ha-ha-ha-ha-ha-ha-ha-ha-ha-ha!'

The problem with making yourself king is that not everyone will believe you should be. Abimelech had a way of dealing with this. If they wouldn't stand for his national anthem he had them bumped off. And even those who at first had wanted him to be king started to think, 'I could do that'. One such man was called Gaal and, having had a fair amount to drink at a particularly good party after an excellent wine harvest he started to say what he was thinking (often very dangerous). Now Zebul was kind of prime minister for Abimelech and

'HIC!'

looked after Shechem for him. Naturally, he was at the party too and wanted to keep on the king's good side (left, right? Who knows?). He rushed to tell him what was going on and suggested that it would be better if Gaal had his mouth shut... permanently! Not surprisingly, Abimelech brought his men to Shechem and when Gaal stepped out of the city gates the next morning, there he was. Suddenly, Gaal wished that last night had been a horrible dream, but his hang-over told him it

wasn't. Not to worry though, Abimelech had plans to cure his headache forever! Fortunately (for him) Gaal managed to escape, but Abimelech had made it clear who was boss.

Unfortunately, if you realise that one person might be after your job, you soon start thinking that there might be others. Of course, not every guilt-ridden self-appointed, king would have dealt with matters quite so drastically as Abimelech. He just waited for the people of the city to come strolling out for a walk and then made sure that they never walked anywhere or did anything else ever again. Abimelech then destroyed the city, poured salt over the land and battered anyone found wandering around. Stories that he was later charged with 'assalt and battery' were just an excuse for a very bad joke.

After this, Abimelech turned his attention to the next city... supposing he had enemies there, too. You can see where this

HERE ABIMELECH! THERE MUST BE A QUICKER WAY OF DOING THIS!

could all end up can't you? Salt, ruined cities, bodies everywhere and nobody left for Abimelech to be king over. But don't worry, this story has a sort-of-happy ending. But not for Abimelech.

He heard that some of Shechem's leaders had escaped to the temple of 'Baal of the covenant' (not a very snappy name I know, but we're dealing with the real world here). Without pausing for breath, Abimelech chopped off the nearest tree-branch, got his soldiers to do the same and arranged them neatly round the temple where these people had the nerve to still be alive. He was going to make a human bonfire, and was just wondering if he could wait the several hundred years it would take for matches to be invented, when somebody passed him a burning branch. In one huge flare up, a thousand people died. Nice, caring sort of guy this king. Just the kind of bloke on whose head you'd drop a millstone if you got the chance and – strangely enough – that's just what happened. Read on, dear reader, and take heart.

By now, Abimelech was seeing enemies everywhere and, knowing that the best enemy is a dead enemy, set off to sort this out. At the next city (Thebez), he was about to burn down the tower where the townspeople had hidden, when the story took a strange turn. One of the women of Thebez had had the foresight to take a millstone up to the top of the tower with her (remember kiddies, never leave home without one).

When she had Abimelech within range (ie right below her) she gave a convincing display of the laws of gravity, aeons before Newton started messing around with apples. Down went the millstone, down went Abimelech beneath it and down went his sense of pride – fancy being beaten by a woman. He did not want the words 'FELLED BY A FEMALE' on his tombstone, so his last words were to ask a passing soldier to finish him off... which he did.

Tyrant, torturer, arrogant, proud, foul-tempered, dead. Choose whichever words you like: they tell you all you need to know about Abimelech. You can hear the whisper going around Israel, 'Oh for a quiet life.' And, as we shall see, that's more or less what they got for the next forty-five years.

JUIR

Judges come, judges go and just in case this is all becoming a little monotonous for you, here's a little riddle to brighten your day.

A judge was going to Gilead
And on his way he met a handsome lad
The lad was his son and so were the others
I should have said he was travelling with his twenty-nine brothers
Now to save their feet from getting dirty
They were riding along on donkeys thirty
So there they all were on the road that day
Count them if you can as they went on their way
Donkeys, and brothers, judge and handsome young lad
Just how many were off to the land of Gilead?

'MINE'S GOT A FITTED MUSIC SYSTEM, GO-FASTER STRIPES, ADDITIONAL OFF-ROAD CAPABILITIES, AIR CONDITIONING AND FURRY DICE!'

ANSWER

Just the one – the judge. All the others were going the other way. The judge was called Jair (pronounced Jay-eer). He really did have thirty sons (ouch, think of the pocket money) and they really did have thirty donkeys (think of the – no, forget it!) and he really did rule for thirty years (well, only twenty-two actually, but it sounded better that way).

JUDGES 10:3-5

JEPHTHAH

It was like half-price day at the pick 'n' mix counter in Israel. Any kind of god was fair game – not just your usual Baal and Astarte, but cheap foreign import gods were flooding the market from Syria, Sidon, Moab, Ammon, Philistia. You name it, the Israelites worshipped it, leaving their own god, the one true God, Lord of Heaven and Earth and constant rescuer of the Israelite nation, completely out of the picture. As a result, as had happened so often before, the people were overthrown and other nations came in to run the country. This time they were Philistines and Ammonites.

Now, if you have been keeping up, you will no doubt

'I DIDN'T EVEN GET TO PUT ON SOME CLEAN UNDIES!'

expect that what happens next is that the Israelites realise they have made a big mistake, say sorry to God, who sighs and says 'OK, I'll

give you another chance,' a major leader emerges and God helps them get rid of the enemy. But not on this occasion. The people pleaded, they made promises, they said how this time it was going to be different, but God just said, 'No, I'm not listening.' In an act of desperation, the Israelites destroyed their false idols and started praying like it was going out of fashion. Now obviously God *was* listening, and he knew when people were just saying one thing and thinking another and when they really meant it. Something about the way things were going on made God realise that *this* time all their pleading and praying was more than words. Perhaps he'd help these needy Israelites again.

Meanwhile, out in the wilderness, a gang of men were sorting out their spoils from their latest raid on the villages round about. These twelfth-century (BC) vagabonds were a sort of Israelite version of Robin Hood and his merry men – except these happy Hebrews, or whatever you like to call them, stole from anyone (not just the rich) and kept it all for themselves. (As they were the poorest people they knew, this seemed fair.) Their leader was Jephthah, hated by his half-brothers, and cast out into the desert by them. Very early on, Jepthah had got the message that his beginnings weren't all they should be. His brothers didn't like him and they let him know

that if he hung around the family home too much he would be late: as in 'the late Jephthah, son of Gilead'. So he had left and taken up with the other regional outcasts, leaving only his reputation for being a bit of a fighter behind him. When it looked like his brothers were about to become the Ammonites'

'DID I SAY "CAST INTO THE DESSERT"? OOPS!'

latest conquest, they thought about Jephthah – not the unpleasant bits but about how good he was in a fight. It became clear that even if people didn't want Jephthah at their dinner parties, and certainly didn't include him on

70

their Happy Hanukkah card lists, he was the one they needed to sort out their current mess.

But Jephthah had his pride and named his terms. 'If I help and we win, then I become the next judge.' His brothers gulped. This went against the grain a bit, but staying alive with him in charge didn't seem so bad when you

considered the alternative. So they agreed and waited for the battle to commence.

Imagine their surprise when Jephthah's first move was to go to talk to the Ammonites instead of opening fire. He

listened to their arguments, considered their claims on the land, weighed up the pros and cons and then said, 'You're wrong,' and proceeded to give them a history lesson. I won't bore you with the details, but it went something like this: 'Israel leave Egypt blah blah blah,

'PAY ATTENTION AND YOU MAY LEARN SOMETHING...'

King of Edom blah blah blah, no way through, king of Moab blah blah blah, detour, more kings, fight, victory, God on our side so watch it pal, blah blah blah.' Now you or I would be convinced by such compelling arguments, but the king of Ammon wasn't impressed.

Jephthah knew he was going to have to fight and was so convinced that God was not going to let him lose he made an incredible (and as it turned out rather foolish) promise. If he won, he would kill the first person to come out of his house when he returned from battle, as a thank-offering to God. At the back of his mind was probably the thought that one of his desert gang would be there to greet him and he could always pick up another one on special offer at Tesco.

Well, God had obviously decided to let the Israelites have another go at getting it right and Jephthah won the

'YES – WE WON THE WAR – DA – YES – WE WON THE WAR – DA– DAR – DA DARR – DA...'

battle. He dashed home to share the good news and rushing to greet him from his doorway was...

'OH NO!'

Rushing to meet him was not some worthless outlaw or ten-a-shekel servant, but his daughter Mizpah. Well, a promise is a promise, as Mizpah well knew. All she asked for was a final couple of months to think of what might have been: she went off into the mountains with her friends and had a bit of a weep and a wail. Now, of course, she could have stayed there, but as she

'... AND THEN WE CAN CHEER-UP WITH SOME ICE CREAM, THEN WE CAN PLAY TWISTER, OH, THEN WE CAN PLAY MURDER IN THE DARK... OOPS! SORRY!'

had already said, a promise is a promise, so eight weeks later she came back to die. Jephthah kept his promise and the people kept theirs, making him leader. Quite a prize, but probably a poor substitute for having your daughter around. He never really got the chance to forget about how stupid he'd been, put it down to experience and move on, as every year, around the anniversary of Mizpah's death, he would come across weeping women reminding him of his daughter – a daughter who knew the cost of obeying God.

MORAL: Be careful what you say – somebody else might not live to regret it.

PS: Jephthah could have settled down for a bit of peace and quiet, but one group was not happy. The people of Ephraim had been left out of the fighting and they wanted to know why. You may recall (see the story of Gideon) that this was a common problem but Jephthah decided to sort it once and for all, rounded up his men and silenced the Ephraimites. A few stragglers were still around, trying to pretend they were anything but Ephraimites. However, Jephthah's men had a clever way to find

74

out the truth. You see, the people of Ephraim couldn't say the letters 'sh', so all you had to do was give them a word with these letters in and watch as they gave themselves away, and then 'shush' them forever.

'IT'S A S-S-S... A LAMB? OR... ERM... A SW-SW-SW...A EWE? A SW-SP-SW... A FARMYARD ANIMAL, MAYBE?... ERM... OH, S-S-SOOGAR!! YOU'VE CAUGHT ME OUT!'

'Shimple!' (As Sean Connery would say!)

JUST A MINUTE...

Now where was I? 'Spin Cycle'. Of course it wasn't 'Spin Cycle', but there is something important going on that gives us the key to all of these stories. It'll come to me, just give me time. Well, by now you're probably getting used to the ways of the Israelites. They choose how they're going to live, find it doesn't work out, so go back to the supplier (ie God) and say let's start again and for a while it works, until the people get fed up or forget what it was like to suffer, and so drift back to their old ways.

It's a bit like going shopping for your mum's Christmas present. You see something you know you've got to have, buy it and when you get home you realise the colours are awful, your mum's allergic to wool and you've spent far too much money. Now, if you have been clever, you will have done your shopping at a place where you can take the green and purple llama wool cardigan back and get something that is more... well, more your mum. One lot of goods is swapped for another. It's not really shopping, it's more like recycling... yeah, that's right, recycling. That's what's going on. The difference is that most recycling is supposed to turn something wrong into something right. Most of the time the Israelites swapped what was wrong for what was wronger... hadn't got the hang of this recycling lark at all.

THE SIN CYCLE

SΛMSON

He was the child they had always wanted. Manoah and his wife thought they would never have children, until the day the 'Angel with no name' appeared. He came from nowhere, and disappeared in a puff of smoke, without eating his dinner, leaving only the message that to them a child would be born, a son given. This is the story of that child. Your mission, should you choose to accept it, is to read this story, think again about the unlikely people God uses, and then have a good look at yourself in the mirror. This story will self-destruct...

The Manoah family were thrilled at the birth of the boy. They named him Samson (which roughly translated means 'little ray of sunshine' – had his parents known what was going to happen they might well have called him 'Stubborn little so and so'). But as they looked at this baby, the future was a long way off. As the 'Angel with no name' had told them, they dedicated

JUDGES
13:1-5

Samson's life to the service of God as a Nazirite. Nazirites were never allowed to cut their hair – good news surely? (Unless you happen to be an Olympic swimmer.) But they weren't allowed to drink alcohol either

78

'TEENAGE HORMONES FOR YOU!' and some said this made his coming of age party a bit of a dull affair. Still, his school chums never argued with him cos this girlie-haired, orange juice drinker was incredibly strong. There were dead lions littered around the country with 'Sam woz 'ere' signs stuck in their heads and as for what he did to foxes – well, members of the 'we love wildlife' club should look away now... He took three hundred foxes, tied their tails together and set fire to them. Everybody was eating roast fox for the next month, but not before the foxes had raced through the harvest fields of the Philistines (Israel's current invaders and public enemy number one) and destroyed the crops. You didn't mess around with Samson.

He was also – well there's no nice way of putting this – a spoiled brat. He knew what he wanted and if he couldn't have it he would stamp, scream and more than likely burn down your orchards. Just like when he wanted to get married. His parents expected him, as someone meant to be serving God, to marry a nice Israelite girl. Imagine their surprise when he told them the girl of his dreams (and

79

their nightmares) was a Philistine. He wouldn't take 'no' for an answer, and it was when his dad saw what he did to one of those lions we mentioned earlier that he finally decided that his boy was not one to argue with. The wedding arrangements were made and Samson threw a party to celebrate his coming marriage to the girl who (like the angel) had no name.[1] As the party went on, people, as they do, started telling jokes and Samson thought of a way to get some clothes and other goods out of the party guests. He was going to tell them a riddle, and if they could solve it he would give them a whole wardrobe of clothes, but if they couldn't answer it Samson would be set up in the gent's outfitting business for life. So here's the riddle:

Riddle me, riddle me, riddle me ree
Out on the road what did I see?
As he looked for food he became something to eat
Strong though he was he produced something sweet.

The Philistines knew there was nothing like a good puzzle, and although this might seem nothing like a good puzzle to you, it had them stumped. The days of the party passed by and they were no nearer finding an answer. They knew that they couldn't afford to give Samson all the clothes they had bet so they had a word with his fiancée – get the answer, they said, or your dad's house will become a giant barbecue. She tried to find out the answer but Samson was giving nothing away, so she turned to the ultimate weapon. She cried and cried and cried until he could stand it no more and told her the answer. I'm not

---

[1] It's true – here's a good party trick. Ask people who Samson's wife was and count how many people say Delilah. But no – Delilah was somebody quite different – as you are about to find out.

going to tell you what it was – read the story yourself or, better still, look on a tin of Golden Syrup... but be warned, it's the sort of riddle that makes Christmas cracker jokes look good. Of course, you can guess the rest – she told the party guests, they told Samson who threw a huge wobbly, said the wedding was off and stormed back home to mummy.

However, a while later when he had calmed down a bit, he went back to say sorry and took his wife-to-be a present – it was a baby goat.[2] But too late! She had married the best man – well, when a girl's splashed out on a dress and your dad's paid for the reception, you can't keep the guests hanging around for Mr Hunk to stop sulking.

Samson was annoyed, well cross – OK, he was furious – and that's when the fox-fire incident took place (we won't go into that again). When the Philistines found out why they weren't going to have their Harvest supper that year (or any other supper for months to come), they looked for someone to blame. So it was that the 'wife with no name' and her dad found out what it was like to be foxes. Burning them didn't give the

---

[2] Hint to young Romeos: don't try this with that girl you keep looking at across the playground. Chocolates, flowers, bubble bath – YES. A copy of this book – DEFINITELY. A baby goat – NO. It will not impress at all and that's the truth, no *kidding*.

Philistines any more food, but the glowing embers kept them warm for a few nights while they planned their next move.

'HEY GUYS! FORGET THE CROPS! WE CAN TOAST THOSE MARSH-MALLOWS NOW!'

Now, just because Samson was cross with the 'wife with no name' (I suppose she could have been known as Mrs Best Man by this time), it didn't mean he didn't love her, and when he heard of her fate he went out and killed a few of the Philistines in return. These things escalate, and soon the Philistines were looking for Samson. The people of Judah just wanted to be left in peace, so they went out to get Samson to hand him over. They tied him with ropes and took him to the town of Lehi, where the Philistine soldiers were waiting, sharpening their swords.[3] They gathered round, trying to decide who was going to strike first, the tension mounted and then, with one

---

[3] The Philistines were very proud of their swords, as they were one of the first nations to discover the secret of making iron weapons.

mighty flex of his biceps, Samson was free (I told you he was strong). Stopping only to pick up a donkey's jawbone lying on the floor, he went ballistic and at the end of the day the score was Samson 1,000 – Philistines 0. Now, all this happened because a few blokes cheated in a joke-telling contest, so just imagine what it would have been like if you had done something really serious, like standing in front of Samson in the 'nine items only' supermarket queue with ten things in your basket.[4]

Suddenly, the people of Judah and the other Israelites did a quick turn around. Forgetting that only moments before they had been handing him over to be killed, they thought, all things considered, he'd be better on their side and so made him their ruler and judge.

The years passed, the Philistines were still there, Samson's hair grew longer. The spring came round and a young man's fancy turned to love (well, Samson's did anyway). He'd wandered over to Gaza – a Philistine city, but Samson's track record was such that nobody was going to tangle with him. Here he found a 'woman with no name – mark II' (what is it about this family?) who threw herself into his arms. Now I don't want to be too indelicate, but I wouldn't want you thinking that this was love at first sight. In fact, this woman was a bit of a one when it came to lads and would throw herself into anybody's arms if they paid

---

[4] Don't you just hate it when that happens?

enough. Well, Samson did do what a man's gotta do and then, just to warn off the Philistines, he stole their city gates and carried them away. But Samson didn't want to get a reputation for kissing and running – besides stealing city gates was only funny the first few times. He wanted someone to adore and respect him for what he was (a self-centred, bad-tempered bozo), someone who could share his leisure pastimes of arson, wildlife destruction and wanton vandalism, someone who would love, honour and obey and particularly obey. He found Delilah and was smitten. She was a Philistine girl, but quite honestly, the only sign of Samson's original promise to serve God was his long hair. All in all, Samson was his own boss and he was making the rules.

The Philistine leaders could hardly believe their luck. They knew Delilah and knew she had a weakness, and it wasn't for long-haired Israelites with an attitude problem. No, Delilah liked the finer things in life and needed the money to buy them. Well, money was no object as far as the nation's leaders were concerned – all she had to do was to find out the secret of Samson's strength and find a way of handing him over as prisoner. Delilah set to work, trying to wheedle the secret out of Samson. She fluttered her eyelashes, called him 'Sammy' and in a voice that had got her

84

everywhere with other blokes said, 'If you really loved your Deely-weely you'd tell me what makes you so strong.'

Samson treated it all as a bit of a joke. 'Tie me up with bowstrings,' he said, 'and I'll be as weak as the next man.' So while he was asleep she did just that, hiding the Philistine soldiers in the next room. They burst out of the room and Samson burst out of the bonds. The soldiers ran and Samson lived to fight another day.

Delilah didn't like being tricked and asked Samson to take her seriously. So, with a straight face, he told her the only way to sap his strength was to tie him with brand new ropes. You can probably guess what happened next – and you'd be right. It was the same when he told her to weave his hair into a loom and no doubt Samson could have gone on playing this game for days ('Dress me in yellow', 'Give me two pillows to sleep with', 'Pour my drinks using your right hand'[5]), the possibilities were endless. But Delilah had neither the time nor the patience, so she turned on the tears (which you might recall had worked on Samson before and worked on him again). Finally exhausted by the weeping, the sleepless nights and the endless nagging, Samson gave in – 'It's my hair,' he said. 'Get rid of that and I'll be

---

[5] Better still use a jug – Heh heh!

completely useless.' A case of hair today – goon tomorrow.

She called in the Philistine leaders one more time, and they watched as Samson fell asleep on Delilah's lap and the barber set to work. He only had one style: number one all over and soon the deed was done.

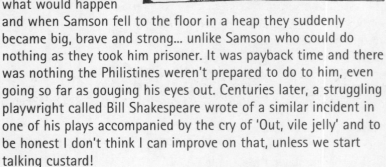

As before, Delilah woke him up, the soldiers waited to see what would happen and when Samson fell to the floor in a heap they suddenly became big, brave and strong... unlike Samson who could do nothing as they took him prisoner. It was payback time and there was nothing the Philistines weren't prepared to do to him, even going so far as gouging his eyes out. Centuries later, a struggling playwright called Bill Shakespeare wrote of a similar incident in one of his plays accompanied by the cry of 'Out, vile jelly' and to be honest I don't think I can improve on that, unless we start talking custard!

Samson, born to be God's servant, had turned away from him so many times, but still God stayed with him. Now, though, with his hair gone, it felt like God had left him too. But God hadn't finished with him yet, even if he felt completely isolated working in the prison grinding corn for his enemies and being brought out on special occasions to be made fun of by the Philistine hordes. They liked to drag him into the centre of the party and ask for some show of strength, finding it incredibly amusing when he couldn't do the stuff. People are so cruel but, as they say in opera

– it ain't over till the blind prisoner sings (or something like that).

It was considered the greatest triumph of the Philistines, to have conquered this unconquerable leader of Israel, and so they had a party to celebrate. The wine flowed, the women danced and suddenly it was cabaret time. Samson was to be the main attraction. A young boy led him to the centre of the temple of

the pagan gods, where he rested against the stone pillars, waiting for the taunts and the insults that were bound to come his way.

Then Samson prayed. It had been a long time since he had talked with God but, as always, God was ready and waiting. Aware of his failings, Samson hardly dared ask for this one last favour but, with stumbling words, he looked for one more chance to be useful in the service of Israel and their God. And, as he loves to do, God answered the prayer. Samson pulled himself up, reached out for the pillars of the temple and pushed. One of the crowd shouted out, 'Hey, baldy, show us what you're made of!' and then there was a sudden silence round the room as people realised that, whatever else they wanted to call him, 'baldy' was not really appropriate any more. Then, breaking the silence, came the sounds of rumbling, splintering and crumbling as the whole temple crashed down on the party-goers. As cabaret-turns go, this one would be talked of in months to come as really bringing the house down – if there had been anybody left to talk about it, but there wasn't.

MICAH, HIS PRIEST AND OTHER LOCAL DIFFICULTIES

JUDGES 17–21

Over three hundred years have gone by since the start of this book (I know, I know, it feels like it. Very funny – look I do the jokes round here, OK?). Joshua died believing he had brought the different tribes into Canaan, where together they could be shaped into one nation, committed to serving God. Well, as we have seen, it didn't quite work out like that. We have considered some of the major leaders – in fact, now I come to think of it, all of the major leaders – but there are more stories to tell. Stories of people realising they have done wrong and trying to put it right, people looking for a place to call their own and stories showing it isn't always easy to do the right thing. Oh yes, you can be sure that to choose the truth will always bring dilemmas and to 'choose God', as Joshua wanted the people to do all those centuries before, is not easy. There isn't time to tell you about everything that happened (besides, we don't know everything that happened) but there are one or two snapshots to give you a sense of some of the problems people faced.

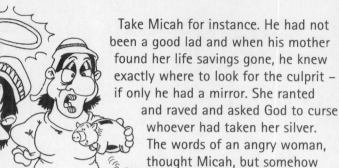

Take Micah for instance. He had not been a good lad and when his mother found her life savings gone, he knew exactly where to look for the culprit – if only he had a mirror. She ranted and raved and asked God to curse whoever had taken her silver. The words of an angry woman, thought Micah, but somehow they were words that kept going round and round in his head. Supposing God really did listen to her and curse the thief, then that would mean he would be cursed, and while he wasn't averse to a bit of cursing on others, this seemed a bit close to home. To sort it out, Micah did what a lot of people have done before or since – he got religious. First of all, though, he gave his mum the money back.

Well, she was chuffed and convinced herself that it must all have been a family misunderstanding. Obviously, she didn't want her son cursed, so she made an idol to try to keep God pleased. How confused can you get? She was typical of many people at the time, who thought God could be bribed with a generous sacrifice or a silver-plated statue, when all he really wanted was for people to listen to him, talk to him

'GOD WILL LOVE IT WHEN WE WORSHIP THIS!'

and let him share their lives. Micah watched his mum and followed suit, building himself a little shrine filled with gods, and even paid one of his sons to be his personal priest. Just when he thought he couldn't improve on this, a Levite came knocking on Micah's door, looking for a bite to eat and a bed for the night. Well, Micah couldn't believe his luck. A real Levite![1] The tribe God had said should be the priests in Israel. This particular Levite hadn't expected Micah to give him a job... but we don't always get what we want in this life.

'THE SACRIFICES I MAKE FOR MY DAD!'

---

[1] 'Reuben was the eldest of the children of Israel', so the song goes, but Levi was number three. God decided that Levi's descendants would have the right to carry out the religious services, perform the sacrifices and make sure that everything God wanted done was carried out. Of course, they weren't all on tabernacle duty... this one was obviously after a bit of freelance work.

'THE JEANS CONFIRM IT! YOU ARE FROM THE TRIBE OF LEVI!!'

Micah went to bed pleased and was sure that God would be too. He's just one example, showing that when we turn away from God and try to work things out for ourselves, no matter how good things look, they can all go horribly wrong.

Then there are the people of Dan. Centuries before, they had been given their bit of the Promised Land – enough room for them all and then some. But, instead of listening to God and

clearing out the Amorites from their territory, they tried to do things their way and found themselves taking refuge in the hills. This was not a satisfactory state of affairs and so they looked around for some land that might be easier to get. The word on the streets (or in this case, in the hills) was that the place to go was 'Oop North', where it might be grim but the people would be easier to conquer. They sent out some spies to check it all out.

On the way, these spies came across Micah's house and noticed that the priest didn't talk like a local. What was he doing

'ERM... YOU'LL BE FINE?'

out here? When they heard about Micah's job creation project for priests in training, they had an idea. Taking the Reverend Levi to one side they asked if he'd be interested in doing a bit of freelance prophesying. The priest was delighted. The spies wanted to know if their journey

would be successful. Now, you don't have to be preacher of the year to work out that what they wanted to hear was 'Yes, of course it will, no problem', so that is exactly what the priest told them (clearly this young man would go far and, as it happened, further than expected).

The spies went on their way and found the town of Laish. It was inhabited by people from Sidon which was a very long way away. They were peaceful people who minded their own business, so the thought that somebody would be interested in disrupting their cosy lives never crossed their minds.

But, as far as the spies were concerned, this was the land they were looking for, and so rushed back home to gather the troops. Of course, on the way back to Laish, they passed Micah's place again and somebody had the bright idea of taking the idols, religious objects and the priest along with them, in the hope that this would mean God was bound to be on their side.

Micah was not best pleased, and he and some of their neighbours chased after the five spies to get their priest back. They reckoned they would be more than a match for five soft southerners. Unfortunately, they hadn't realised that the five soft southerners had brought six hundred tough friends with them... Micah made his excuses and left.

There was no fight in Laish, no struggle to the end as the townsfolk defended their property. The army of Dan just moved in, said 'we're in charge now' and changed the name of the town to Dan (they weren't a particularly original bunch).

Well, they had their land, but it wasn't where God wanted them to be, and still there were all these idols and false gods all over the

place – the very first things they had been told to get rid of. Unbelievable, but it seemed to be the history of the nation from start to finish and, if we're honest, our lives are a bit like that too, aren't they? Go on admit it –

94

when was the last time you made a new year resolution that you kept? Or how often do you learn about the things God wants you to do and then spend the rest of the day looking for a way round them? Hmmm?

Here's one more story of a nation in pieces when, with a bit of faith and commitment, they could have been top country. Listen carefully, while I relate the tale of the wife who ran away and then found herself without a leg or anything else to stand on, let alone run on.

Well, this particular woman decided she'd had enough of being a Levite's partner and ran back home to daddy. It wasn't long before her husband came to retrieve her. It took him several days before daddy let his little girl go again; there was always some reason for staying, but in the end he had to put his foot down with a firm hand and nsist that they left. By the time they got away it was getting late, and finding somewhere to stay the night was top priority. An old farmer saw them struggling along and offered them hospitality for the night.

Unfortunately, not everyone in the town where he lived was quite so welcoming: the local Benjaminites surrounded the house, wanting the visitor to come out. Suspecting that they weren't going to suggest a quiet game of snakes and ladders, the husband stayed where he was. But when

they wouldn't take no for an answer, he threw his poor wife outside instead (who says chivalry is dead? I do!). They taunted her, they beat her, they abused her and when they'd had enough, they left her on the doorstep for the husband to find in the morning. He was up early, keen to be home before dark. Not so the lady on the doorstep. She wouldn't be going anywhere ever again.

Well, he could have given her a decent burial, nice gravestone, a bit of a tea for the family afterwards. He didn't of course – that would be too normal. Instead he chopped her up into twelve bits – one for each tribe – and sent them out to show what a terrible thing had happened. It can be quite traumatic to open your post at breakfast and have a leg or half a head drop out on your plate, so the tribes were determined that such a thing was never going to happen again. They gathered together to make sure the Benjaminites learned a lesson they would never forget.

The Benjaminites could see the soldiers gathered near the city wall and, on the basis that you should do unto others before they do you, they went out and attacked – leaving the city defenceless. So, while they were out the front door, 10,000 soldiers from the other tribes nipped in round the back. The city was theirs and the people of Benjamin were thoroughly defeated. Even the ones outside the front gate who made a run for it weren't running for very long, although a few hid out in the hills, hoping to escape detection.

But this is where the dilemma occurs. The tribe of Benjamin, for all its faults and wrongdoings, was one of the twelve tribes. The eleven other tribes had, on the one hand, avenged an evil deed but they might have wiped out one twelfth of God's people, which didn't seem quite right. Their solution was unusual. Having discovered that the people of Jabesh had taken no part in the fighting, they went out and killed all the men of the tribe, taking the women and girls of Jabesh prisoner. These were then

'LET'S MAKE BABIES THEN! SHUCKS, IT'S A HARD JOB BUT SOMEBODY'S GOT TO DO IT.'

offered to the Benjaminites who still remained, so
they could have more Benjaminite babies. And
just in case this wasn't enough, the men of
Benjamin were also told they could
have their pick of the dancing girls of
Shiloh. So honour was satisfied, a
tribe was rescued from extinction
and all seemed well, but you can't
help feeling that if only they'd paid
more attention to God in the first
place, they wouldn't have ended up
with all this inter-tribal fighting, pretend
priests, idol worship and carved-up
women on the doorstep. The history of
Israel during the time of the judges is
summed up in the last sentence of the
book:

'Everyone did just as he pleased'
... and it couldn't go on like this.

RUTH

As we get ready to leave Judges and peek into what was round the corner for God's people, I don't want you to go away with the idea that this was a nation whose history was littered with left-handed, double-dealing, cowardly, deceitful, rash-promise-making, fox-burning heroes. It might not seem like it, but there was actually more to the country than that. There were good, selfless, dedicated, committed people, and this is the story of one of them (as you will discover, she was a foreigner, but good people in Israel were hard to find).

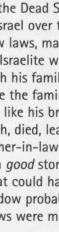

Ruth

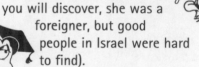

Ruth lived in the land of Moab, a country on the other side of the Dead Sea, that had had its difficulties with Israel over the years. She was, despite the Hebrew laws, married to Mahlon, an Israelite who had moved with his family to Moab to escape the famine in Egypt. Mahlon, like his brother Chilion and his father Elimelech, died, leaving Ruth and Orpah with their mother-in-law (no cheap jokes please, this is a *good* story). If dying was the worst thing that could happen to you, then being left a widow probably came a close second – widows were mistreated, swindled

Orpah

100

Naomi

and often
ignored.
With their
husbands
out of the
way, they
were
considered
easy prey

for the unscrupulous (and, as
we have discovered, there
were a lot of those in Israel). But God had thought of this, and the
Israelite law gave other members of the family the responsibility
of caring for the widows.

'THEY MAKE FINE
COFFEE TABLES... OR
MAYBE A DOORMAT?'

Unfortunately for Elimelech's widow, Naomi, her family were back
in Judah. When the news came through that the harvest had been
good and there was food available, Naomi decided to go back and
look for help and support from her family there. Orpah and Ruth
came with her but, thinking they needed to be with their own
people, Naomi told them to go back. Orpah accepted the offer, but
Ruth would not go and said something that centuries later still
makes the hair stand up on the back of your neck and a shiver run
down your spine (well it does me anyway):

'Where you go, I will go, and where you stay, I will stay. Your people will be my people and your God my God.'

Ruth was prepared to turn her back on all the things she knew – her family and friends, her way of life and worship – because Naomi was her family now and she was not going to abandon her.

They settled in Bethlehem (at last, a place we've heard of) during harvest time. There was always corn and grain left over at the edges of fields and the poor people, eg the widows, were allowed to go and collect this for themselves. Ruth went to get corn for her and Naomi, and she worked and worked and worked. The owner of the fields, Boaz, a relative of Naomi, saw Ruth and offered her his protection, the right to collect corn from the best parts of the field and even invited her to lunch. He said it was her reputation that made him do all this, but those watching suspected that there was something else going on (and yes, this is going to get slushy).

Naomi was excited by all that was going on and, thinking that her daughter-in-law ought to be married again, she began looking round for a suitable man. Of course, she didn't have to look far to see Boaz. She formed a plan.

DEUTERONOMY
25:5-10

We have already said that family members were expected to take care of widows. The laws of Deuteronomy said that the nearest male relative could marry the widow. If they did, they would be called the 'kinsman redeemer' (or KR for short). They could, of course, say no and then the next nearest male relative could choose and so on and so forth, like a big game of pass the family

'THAT WAS A FEELING IN MY LOINS, NOT MY LIONS!'

parcel. However, Naomi had a feeling in her water (whatever that means) that the game would end long before the music stopped.

Like many things, there was a little ritual to go through if you wanted to tell the relative that a) you were available (in the nicest possible sense); and b) you were claiming their care and protection. What you did was go into where the chap was sleeping (in this case Boaz) and sleep at his feet. Now I know what I'd do if somebody came into my bedroom in the middle of the night and offered themselves as a human hot-water bottle and it involves loud screams, sucking the corner of the duvet and shouting to my wife 'Help!!!' but, believe me, in those days it was quite the done thing.

'ARGGHHH!'

So Ruth set off to do this and quietly lay down to sleep at the foot of Boaz's bed. It was about midnight when he woke up and realised that his feet were warm and there was Ruth. You could have knocked him down with a feather (except he was already lying down). Now Boaz was not, as they say, in the first flush of youth

'AHHH! HIDE THE FALSERS!'

and was flattered that Ruth should be prepared to come to him when looking for a husband. He would have jumped at the chance and this story could have ended with wedding bells, the

104

throwing of confetti and a warm feeling all round. But, as with all good romances (and this is one of the best), there was a hitch to them getting hitched and Boaz was too honest a man to keep quiet about it.

You see, although he was a *close* relative of Naomi's, he wasn't the closest. There was somebody else who ought to have the right of first refusal on Ruth (I know this all sounds a bit like a cattle market with the women as prize exhibits, but I'm only telling the story and that's the way it was). But Boaz was in love and he wasn't going to give up Ruth if he could help it. He packed her off back to Naomi with a load of barley to keep them going and set off to put things right.

'IT'S NOT A WEDDING RING IS IT!'

BARLEY

The relative was by the city gate, which was where you gathered if you wanted to know what was what, who was who and why was why.[1]

He had the right to buy all Elimelech's property and, in these unequal opportunity days, that included Naomi and Ruth too, but

[1] Where they gathered in Gaza once Samson had pinched the gates, I have no idea. Details, details always details.

he wasn't keen. 'She's yours if you want her, and all the land,' he said. If he wanted? If he wanted! As if Boaz had wandered out early in the morning simply for a chance of a gossip and an opportunity to reflect on the inheritance laws. The deal was sealed, and if you think all that business about sleeping at each other's feet was weird wait till you hear how they did business.

If you were selling, you passed over your sandal to the buyer and if witnesses saw you, then it was a done deal. This meant you had to be very careful if someone asked you to pass your slippers, as you could find yourself handing over your land and money with the footwear (still, worth a try, I'd have thought!).

The rest you can work out for yourself. Boaz married Ruth, the mother-in-law came to live with them and they still lived happily ever after! However, as if a story of a foreigner showing God's people how to act with faithfulness and integrity was not strange enough, there is a twist to this tale – Ruth had a baby. Nothing strange in that. She called him Obed – nothing too strange in that, I suppose. The twist is that Obed's grandson (and therefore Ruth's great grandson) became one of the most famous kings of Israel – King David. And his great great great... etc, etc grandson was also born in Bethlehem, and I expect you know all about him.

THINK CHRISTMAS, THINK ANGELS, THINK "AWAY IN MANGER". NOW DO YOU KNOW WHO WE'RE ON ABOUT?'

Of course, those of you who have been keeping up will by now be saying (and if you're not you should be) 'How did they get to have a king? Wasn't God dead against the idea? What happened?' Well, such questions bring us to our concluding pages, as we discover what happened when the time of the judges came to an end and a new chapter began. Read on...

ELI

Eli loved to serve God. Over the years in the temple at Shiloh, although the tribes often ignored God completely, Eli was there making the sacrifices, praying for his people and looking forward to a time when the nation of Israel really would be a bright light shining for the glory of God in a world of darkness. Even when he was older and his sons, Hophni and Phineas, took

over the temple services, Eli liked to keep an eye on what was going on. Which was how he came to be in the temple one evening and caught sight of a woman in the shadows. She was twisting and turning, with her mouth working away like mad but no sound coming out. 'Obviously drunk,' thought Eli and went over to have words with her. But Hannah (the woman in the shadows) was not drunk, just desperately crying out to God with

such anguish that words didn't seem to be enough. When he had come closer, Eli could see that here was a person in real need. He didn't ask what it was she wanted, but simply prayed that God would answer her prayer.

108

Hannah wanted a baby more than anything else. Israelite tradition said a childless woman was a failure, and the law said a man could divorce a wife who had no children. Hannah's husband, Elkanah, stayed faithful, but no matter how often he told Hannah that he would never abandon her – children or no children – something inside her made her desperate for a child. So desperate that she made a promise to God: if you give me a child I will give him back to you, to be your servant for ever. Now, making promises to God is a risky business, as he might take you up on it – as Hannah found out.

The baby, when he came, was everything Hannah had dreamed of. She called him Samuel, a name which means 'God's answer', because God had truly answered her prayers. But now her promise had to be kept – she cared for Samuel until he was about three, and then took him back to Shiloh and looked for Eli. He could just about remember the strange praying woman, but imagine his surprise when she gave him her son to be his helper. A woman who kept her promises – maybe there was hope for the people of Israel after all, thought Eli. Such commitment and faithfulness was in sharp contrast

to his own sons, who were taking the best bits of the sacrifices for themselves, and chatting up any attractive women who happened to come along to the services. He tried to make them face up to their evil, but he was an old man. Who would listen to him?

One person who did listen was Samuel. He worked hard, watched how Eli lived and tried his best to be a good servant of the temple and of God. At night time he would sleep with the door open, just in case Eli needed anything, and so wasn't surprised to wake up one night to hear his name being called.

He rushed in to Eli to see what he wanted. But Eli was fast asleep, and only half-wakened by Samuel, told him to go back to bed, he didn't need him. The second time it happened, he was a little less understanding. By the third time, it occurred to Eli that if *he* wasn't shouting out in his sleep, maybe *God* was.

'If it happens again,' he told Samuel, 'ask God what he wants,' adding to himself as he rolled over, 'and for goodness sake let me get some sleep.' Sure enough, the call came again, and this time Samuel listened to God and didn't much like what he heard.

The next day he tried to avoid Eli, and when he couldn't, talked about all kinds of things and not the happenings of the previous night. He really didn't want to share the message. Eventually, Eli caught up with him and, quite reasonably, wanted to know what God had said.

The message had been about the sins of Eli's sons, and the weakness of Eli in allowing it all to go unchallenged. God had said there would be a price to pay for Eli's family. To Samuel's surprise, Eli didn't get angry or tell him he didn't know what he was talking about. He just said words to the effect that yes, he'd expected it would all come to that.

It hadn't been an easy time for Samuel, but he learned a useful lesson. If we listen, God will speak to us, and the things he says are worth listening to. As Samuel grew, God spoke to him more and more often. He became the sort of young man that people went to for advice, and as he grew older, God began to use him to bring his messages to the people.

Meanwhile, the Israelites continued to be at war – at the moment it was with the Philistines. At a desperate moment in the battle, the soldiers wanted proof that God was with them, and so sent for the ark of the covenant, the special ceremonial box containing the commandments given by God to Moses. The rule was that this ark should always stay in the holiest part of the temple, but Eli's sons had paid little attention to any of the other rules, so why should they bother about this one? So they didn't. It seems that you can only push God so far, and Hophni and Phinehas had reached the limit. Thousands of Israelites were killed in the following battle, and those thousands included the renegade sons of Eli. Worse was to come – the Philistines captured the ark. The visible symbol of how God had called and committed himself to a particular people was in the enemy camp.

Eli, now blind and very old, was waiting for news from the battlefront. He was scared – the ark should not have been moved, nothing good would come of this. When a messenger arrived, he was saddened to hear of the thousands dead, he was grief-stricken to hear of the end of his sons, evil though they were, but nothing could have prepared him for the news of the capture of the ark. It was all too much – he fell off his bench, broke his neck and died. Forty years of leading the people, forty years of praying and watching for God to sort things out, forty years and what was there to show for it? A captured ark, a bloody battlefield, an old man dead on the floor... oh yes, and Samuel.

SAMUEL

The war with the Philistines continued. The ark of the covenant was soon returned, when the Philistines discovered it was more

trouble than it was worth, causing plagues, tumours, spots and other nasty things: all because they had stolen God's ark and he

wasn't too pleased. However, what didn't come back for the Israelites was the sense of being God's people. It had taken a while (centuries actually), but slowly the realisation dawned that what God was interested in was not whether or not they had the right kind of religious objects (like an ark for example), but whether or not they had the right kind of commitment to him as their God. It was time to put things right, and Samuel was the one to right them.

It was quite simple, he told them. All they had to do was do what they should have done in the first place. Get rid of all the false gods, idols and other pagan tat that was littering the land like a school playground on car boot sale day, and put God first, not just in their worship but in every aspect of their lives. When he saw they meant business, he took them to Mizpah and prayed for them, sacrificing a lamb while they fasted (and believe me if the smell of roast lamb while you're starving yourself isn't a test of your commitment, I don't know what is).

'NOTHING LIKE THE SMELL OF ROAST LAMB!'

The Israelites said 'Amen' and looked up. They were completely surrounded by the Philistines. This was it, then. No

more last chances. Suddenly God spoke with a voice that roared across the valleys, scaring the life out of the Philistines and causing a few raised eyebrows among the Israelites too. The Philistines ran. The Israelites ran faster. The Philistines fought. The Israelites fought harder. The Israelites won. The Philistines didn't.

It was a new beginning. The people made Samuel their leader, and for years he judged the country wisely. He made good decisions, he brought the different tribes closer together and, above all, he made sure that God was not pushed to the backs of their minds or kept for special Sabbath services. But even a man like Samuel couldn't go on for ever, and as he got older he began to think about staying in bed in the mornings, reminiscing with his mates down the 'Tent Peg and Mallet' about the good old days, and generally just enjoying life.

So Samuel retired and made his two lads judges in his place. But it wasn't the same. Of course, old people always think things aren't the same, but this time it wasn't Samuel doing the complaining, it was the Israelites.

Samuel used to take the services, but his sons took the offering (literally). In court, Samuel would listen carefully and make the right and just

'SO WHAT ARE YOU WILLING TO PAY TO WIN?'

decision, while his sons would simply say 'He who pays wins'. The Israelites weren't prepared to lose the good things they had gained after all this time, so the leaders of the tribes came to Samuel with an idea.

'WOULD YOU LIKE TO OFFER ANYTHING ELSE TO ME... ER... GOD?'

Samuel sat and listened, waiting for them to name their choice as the new judge of the nation; but when he heard what they had got to say, he nearly fell off his bench. However, he remembered just in time what had happened to Eli when he did that, and he got a grip (on himself and the bench).

118

The people wanted a king. Samuel's heart sank. Had they learned nothing after all this time? God was their king, wasn't that enough? Apparently not. All the other nations had kings, so they wanted one too.

Samuel went to talk to God about it. God wasn't in the least bit surprised (that's the trouble with being omniscient – there are no little twists and turns in life's pattern that can take you unawares). He told Samuel to give them what they wanted, but to remind them that there would be a price to pay. A king would have complete control. The people would have to serve him with no say one way or the other. He would be entitled to the best of their goods and crops. He would rule them, not lead them, and there was a difference. 'Tell them,' said God, 'it will all end in tears.'

Samuel told them, but they weren't listening. Already in their own minds they were planning lavish coronation services,

commemorative plates and looking forward to the first royal garden party.

Some time later, a good looking young man called Saul came to see Samuel because his uncle's donkeys had gone missing. He thought this prophet might be able to find them for him. Samuel was waiting for him – God had told him he was coming. 'Yes, yes I know, the donkeys,' said Samuel, as Saul came running up. 'Don't worry about them – it's all sorted. What's more important is that you are to be the king of Israel.' Saul stared open-mouthed. He rubbed his hand over several days growth of beard, looked at the state of his clothes – dirty and torn after the long journey – sniffed the air and thought it was well past his bath time. 'You must have the wrong man,' he said. Samuel cast his mind back over the years. He couldn't think of an occasion when he had been wrong before, so didn't think it was likely now. He invited Saul to stay and eat, offering him the best slice of meat. 'Er, this isn't donkey is it?' asked Saul. Samuel was beginning to get tired of this. 'Look, the donkeys are fine and you are to be king. Now shut up and eat up!'

The next day, as Saul was leaving, Samuel poured oil over his head and said again, 'You are to be king'. He told him to travel home, and on his way he would meet people with goats, bread and wine. He was to take the bread off them and travel on until he met the prophets coming singing and dancing down the hillside. 'Then,' said Samuel, 'you will know I am not making it all up.'

It all happened just as Samuel said, and Saul never felt the same again. Interestingly enough, Saul was a

Benjaminite, and we've already seen what kind of people they were. But once again, God chooses who he chooses, and he does seem to know best.

Meeting the people was, however, a bit daunting. Samuel gave him a big build up, there was a bit of a fanfare and... nothing. They eventually found Saul. He was hiding in the luggage, hoping he'd be packed away without anyone noticing.

'LADIES AND GENTLEMEN... HE'S A GREAT PERSONAL FRIEND OF MIND, AND A SMASHIN' LAD TO BOOT... KING SAUL... ERM... SAUL?'

'HIS MICROPHONE'S NOT WORKING!'

'WELL, NO ONE'S INVENTED SPEAKERS YET!'

Not a chance – the people wanted a king, and Saul was favourite for the job.

The cry went up around the hills, 'Long live the king!', and so the time of the judges came to an end. The people had got what they wanted, but was it what they really needed? Well, that, as they say, is another story for another day.

LAST BITES

Spin cycle, recycle, what nonsense I talk at times. Man Utd will never win a match again – there's some more. There is something important I want you to get hold of – it just escapes me for the moment.

Let's think back. The stories I have told you follow a familiar pattern. The people ignore God until everything goes wrong. They suffer under foreign invaders and go back to God wanting to start again. God – 'cos that's the kind of guy he is – provides them with a leader to get them out of the mess. Not always the clean-cut, never-done-wrong, credit-to-the-nation type, but often more of your cowardly, double-crossing, bad-tempered, handy-with-a-mallet kind of hero. But the peace, however long it lasts, eventually evaporates in another cloud of 'Let's do it our way' kind of thinking. There seems no end to it, just a continual round of sin – suffer – salvation – sin – suffer – salvation – sin – suffer... you get the idea. A cycle of disobedience and wrongdoing, to which there seems to be no end.

Cycle... hold on it's coming back to me... recycle, bi-cycle, spin cycle... sin cycle!

SIN CYCLE

That's the problem. The whole of Judges describes the sin cycle from which there appears to be no escape. For many of us today, we recognise this pattern in our own lives. We do things we know we shouldn't, we feel bad about it, we make promises to God about how things are going to be different from now on, but they rarely are. We seem stuck in our own endless sin cycle, pedalling nowhere.

But remember, the book of Judges is just one part of the whole Bible which tells a much bigger and better story. God knew that what people needed was not more rules and encouragement to have another go. They needed the ability to get off their bikes (as it were), leave them behind and start travelling in a new direction. Not only did he know that, but he promised to do something about it:

'I will give you a new heart and a new mind. I will take away your stubborn heart of stone and give you an obedient heart. I will put my spirit in you...'

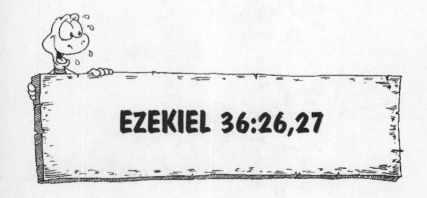

EZEKIEL 36:26,27

God's promise, through Ezekiel, was a promise that things don't always have to be the same – but the change would come not because of what we do, but because of what God did. When the time was right, God came to this earth as a baby. Growing up, he experienced all the difficulties, hard times, pain and temptations that face people the world over – but he didn't give in to them. He then allowed himself to be put to death, not for the things *he'd* done wrong, but for our sin, and to show he was the real winner. Even though many had seen him dead and buried, three days later he was back again, and thousands more saw him and millions in the centuries that followed experienced the new start that he offered them. This is the big story of the Bible. The story of Jesus – Immanuel, God with us. Judges shows us how much we need someone to rescue us – the story of Jesus shows us God's perfect rescue plan. You can read it for yourself. Four friends of Jesus wrote down their versions of his life story – Matthew, Mark, Luke and John. You'll find their books in the New Testament part of the Bible. It really is the best story of all – a story that could change your life... if you let it!

WHO ARE THESE GUYS?

MALC'

Schools-worker, charity coordinator, youth pastor, local radio celebrity, church minister are just some of the 'work experience' that Malc' can fill in on a CV. He has also, at different times, had an ear pierced and dyed his hair green. He devours books, films and black coffee in between working for a church in Coventry, studying in Oxford and socialising with anyone who will talk to him. He has written for SU's *Quest* Bible notes and *SALT* material and now, of course, the blockbuster *Bible Bites* series.

IAN

Shropshire lad, Ian, was born and brought up on a small sheep farm. His childhood dislike of the outdoors, lack of computer games, the everlasting rain and his phobia of chickens (linked to a vicious attack by 300 manic hens when he was four) led him to the drawing board and he's been drawing ever since. Despite his early acquaintances being mainly of the four-legged variety, Ian has progressed through a variety of academic institutions and is now a trainee solicitor working in Sheffield, where he worships at St Thomas's Church.

READY FOR ANOTHER BITE?!!

A giant,
a crown and an
open-air bath

A ladder, a
bbq and a pillar of
salt

A red sea, a burning bush
and a plague of frogs